Contents

À la claire fontaine
(There by the crystal fountain)

Trad. French Canadian
arr. BOB CHILCOTT

OXFORD

Bob Chilcott

Jazz Folk Songs

for Choirs

9 songs from around the world
for mixed voices and jazz trio or piano solo

Bass part

OXFORD
UNIVERSITY PRESS

Great Clarendon Street, Oxford OX2 6DP, England
198 Madison Avenue, New York, NY 10016, USA

Oxford University Press is a department of the University of Oxford.
It furthers the University's aim of excellence in research, scholarship,
and education by publishing worldwide

Oxford is a registered trade mark of Oxford University Press
in the UK and in certain other countries

1 3 5 7 9 10 8 6 4 2

ISBN 978-0-19-336181-2

Music origination by Enigma Music Production Services, Amersham, Bucks.
Printed in Great Britain on acid-free paper by
Halstan & Co. Ltd., Amersham, Bucks.

Sakura
(Cherry tree)

Trad. Japanese
arr. BOB CHILCOTT

Scarborough Fair

Trad. English
arr. BOB CHILCOTT

Tell my ma

Children's song from Northern Ireland
arr. BOB CHILCOTT

The House of the Rising Sun

Trad. American
arr. BOB CHILCOTT

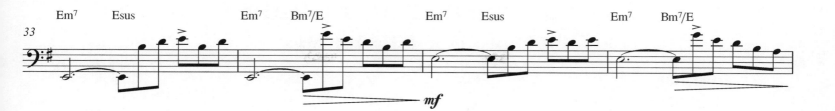

Tuoll' on mun kultani
(There is my loved one)

Trad. Finnish
arr. BOB CHILCOTT

*If the repeat is made the choir should re-enter at bar 23.

Waltzing Matilda

Trad. Australian
arr. BOB CHILCOTT

*If the repeat is made the choir should re-enter at bar 60.

ISBN 978-0-19-336181-2

FOUR CORONATION ANTHEMS

G. F. HANDEL

Anthem I
Zadok the priest

Printed in Great Britain

OXFORD UNIVERSITY PRESS, MUSIC DEPARTMENT, GREAT CLARENDON STREET, OXFORD OX2 6DP